# VISUAL WORDS AND IDIOMS

# Word Bogglers

BANANA

Written by Dianne Draze
Illustrated by Mary Lou Johnson

Prufrock Press Inc.
P.O. Box 8813
Waco, TX 76714-8813
Phone: (800) 998-2208
Fax: (800) 240-0333
http://www.prufrock.com

## What Are Word Bogglers?

Are you looking for a motivating way to combine problem solving, visual discrimination, and language? **Word Bogglers** is just the thing. A word boggler is a puzzle, a brain-teaser, and a lesson in language, all rolled into one.

Each word boggler is a word or phrase that has been written so that its meaning is conveyed via the position, number or size of the words and letters. Some of the puzzles are words and some are familiar idioms and cliches. Thus, it is an opportunity to develop vocabulary and knowledge of often-used phrases in the form of motivating brain-teasers.

Kids are usually fascinated with the way ideas are presented in two-dimensional formats. You will often see students doodling, trying out various styles of writing and writing words to look like their meaning (writing "neon" like **NEON**, "fancy" like fancy, "China" like CHINA, and "fat cat" like **fat cat**). Therefore, **Word Bogglers** taps a natural interest in words and their graphic representation. **Word Bogglers** allows you to use this natural interest to shapen visual thinking skills and develop knowledge of language usage.

## Visual Clues

The clue to solving each word boggler is looking at the way that the words are written in the box. After students have done a few of these puzzles, they will see a pattern that will enable them to solve other word bogglers. Some of the patterns that they will detect are:

- Words that are written at the top of the box usually mean "high" or "top;" such as *high hat* or *top heavy*.
- Words that are written at the bottom of the rectangle usually mean "low" or "bottom;" such as *low ball* or *bottom line*.
- Words that are written vertically from top to bottom mean "down;" such as *downpour, downcast,* or *go down*. Whereas, words that are written vertically from bottom to top have the word "up" in them. They include terms like *upbringing, shape up,* or *look up*. Phrases that have the letters of the words written on a diagonal, either going from top to bottom or bottom to top, will usually include words like "rising," "falling," "downhill" or "uphill." Phrases of this sort include *sunrise, falling prices, waterfall, rising tide,* or *downhill skiing*.

- Words written on the right or left side of the rectangle will have the terms "right," "left" or "side" in them. These include phrases like *right handed, left field* or *side saddle*.

- Words written in big bold letters will have some word in the phrase that means the same as "big," while words that are written very small will include terms like "little," "small," or "tiny." These include phrases like *big shot, small change,* and *little white lie*.

- Sometimes the number of the words or letters is significant. For instance, *fourteen* would be "teen" written four times, *bicycle* would be represented by the word "cycle" written twice, and *parakeet* would be two "keets" (a pair of keets).

- Some words are cut in such a way to indicate they include the words "half" or "split." This would include phases like *lickety split* and *half-hearted*.

- The positioning of words in relation to other words in the rectangle can also give clues to the word phrases. Words written above or below other words usually include the words "above," "under," "over" or "below" in them. These include phrases like *hitting below the belt, feeling under the weather, man overboard,* and *head over heels*. Likewise, words that are written within other words usually include the term "in." These are phrases like *Alice in Wonderland* or a *bird in the hand*. Puzzles that have one word written before or after another word will indicate the words "before" or "after" as a part of the phrase. These include *calm before the storm* or *life after death*.

- Some word bogglers use a combination of these techniques. For instance, the term *falling to pieces*, uses a numeric clue (the word "pieces" written twice) and a positioning clue (the letters are written on a diagonal, indicating falling).

Students must use creative thinking and draw on their knowledge of the English language to solve these word puzzles. The puzzles at the beginning of the book are presented in such a way that the meaning is more obvious than the ones at the end of the book. For instance, if one word is written within another word, the two words are written in different type, so it is easy to see where one word ends and another word begins. These clues are given only for the first few times a concept is introduced. Eventually the letters for both (or all) the words are written together with no differentiation to show where one word ends and the other word begins. This is a much more challenging puzzle for students to decode. If you have children with perception or learning problems, you may wish to rewrite these harder phrases to more clearly show each word.

## Should You Help or Provide Clues?

Part of the fun and challenge of solving any puzzle is struggling with it until you finally are able to unlock the secret and arrive at a solution. If the phrases being depicted are not immediately obvious, let students work on them for a while. Only after providing adequate incubation time should you provide a hint.

## Definitions

At the bottom of each page are definitions of the words and phrases and also lines on which students can write their answers. You can choose to use these definitions in couple of different ways:

- The definitions can be given to students at the same time the word bogglers are presented. In this case, they can be used as clues to help students decipher the puzzles.
- The definitions can also be presented after students have solved the word puzzles and, thereby, used to reinforce their knowledge of the definitions of these phrases.

Since we often use phrases without knowing exactly what we are saying, these definitions can serve the useful function of building knowledge of common word usage.

A logical extension and way to further reinforce the understanding of each phrase would be to have students refer to the definition and then use the phrases in a written sentence. Using *Word Bogglers* this way gives you a unique way to provide a short daily writing experience.

## Suggested Uses

There are several ways that you can use these puzzles in your classroom. Some of the possible uses are:

- Put a word boggler on the overhead each day for a quick, daily thinking challenge. This is a good thing to do at the beginning of class to give students something constructive to do during those first few minutes.
- Use them as starting points for daily writing exercises by having students use the word or phrase in a sentence after they have decoded the word boggler.
- Give students an entire page of word bogglers for a weekly challenge.
- Have students work in groups to solve the brain-teasers. Discuss how each group solved the puzzles.
- Cut up the words bogglers and put them in a learning center or in a box for an enrichment activity.
- Ask students to make up their own puzzles. When you have enough puzzles, put them together in a worksheet.

flight

blue*once*moon

L
O
W

Q P Q P
Q P Q P
P Q Q
Q P P P

LUNCH

**mi**bear**nd**

1. _____  the best; first-rate

2. _____  very rarely

3. _____  facts or secret information

4. _____  manners, as in mind your . . .

5. _____  something for carrying your lunch

6. _____  to remember and think about

**shot**

*machine*

hay*needle*stack

*wish*
star

S
R
I
A
T
S

**cream**

1. _____   an important person
2. _____   a machine to join fabric together
3. _____   something that is hard to find
4. _____   your dreams may come true
5. _____   an upper story or floor of a building
6. _____   a sweet, cold treat

Name _____

<table>
<tr><td>

**tail**

</td><td>

gun salute   gun salute   gun salute
gun salute   gun salute   gun salute
gun salute   gun salute   gun salute
gun salute   gun salute   gun salute
gun salute   gun salute   gun salute
gun salute   gun salute   gun salute
gun salute   gun salute   gun salute

</td></tr>
<tr><td>

*GO*
**board**

</td><td>

dimensional
dimensional

</td></tr>
<tr><td>

BANANA
BANANA

</td><td>

l e g g e d
l e g g e d

</td></tr>
</table>

1. _____  scurry off or leave quickly

2. _____  an official tribute

3. _____  to do too much or be extravagant

4. _____  having length and width but no depth

5. _____  an ice cream concoction

6. _____  sitting with one leg over the other

**corn**
*cob*

m
a
r
k
e
d

dogyou'rehouse

**pressure**
**break**

his eyes his stomach

storm

1. _____    corn in its natural state

2. _____    on sale

3. _____    to be in trouble

4. _____    to fall apart

5. _____    took more than he could eat

6. _____    a winter storm

Name _____

| | |
|---|---|
| **troualwaysble** | *strung* |
| **ꓘƆAꓐ BACK** | *pancakes*<br>*pancakes*<br>*pancakes*<br>*pancakes* |
| cute<br>    cute | **shoulder** |

1. _____  continually doing the wrong thing

2. _____  nervous and tense

3. _____  adjacent or following immediately

4. _____  something you'd eat for breakfast

5. _____  extremely attractive

6. _____  to snub or ignore

**walk**
*eggs*

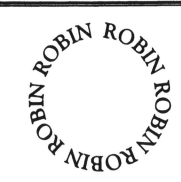

E
L
D
D
A
S

cycle **cycle**

**cycle**

**cycle**

*wonderaliceland*

**what's**
*your mind*

1. _____ to be very cautious

2. _____ to take turns in a circle

3. _____ get ready to go

4. _____ a child's vehicle

5. _____ a classic tale by Lewis Carroll

6. _____ What are you thinking about?

Name _____

| | |
|---|---|
| women |  |
| cajustse | fire<br>**COURAGE** |
| ***BEN*** |  |

1. _____ a novel by Louisa May Alcott
2. _____ emotional pain
3. _____ in the event that; if
4. _____ bravery during times of great trouble
5. _____ a famous clock in London
6. _____ just barely getting away

taking
**BIG**

**ho    ho**

*hand*

cairs

DANCE **DANCE** DANCE
**DANCE** **DANCE**

R
E
E
H
C

1. _____     a large, important project

2. _____     " . . . It's off to work we go."

3. _____     the hand most people write with

4. _____     a party game

5. _____     a dance for four couples

6. _____     to make someone feel better

Name _____

QUARTER (reversed)

WALK WALK WALK WALK WALK WALK BLOCK WALK WALK WALK WALK WALK WALK WALK WALK

habirdnd

flake

skating
(underlined above and below)

word
word word
word
word
word

1. _____ a football player
2. _____ a way to exercise
3. _____ is worth two in the bush
4. _____ a cold, feathery crystal
5. _____ rollerblading
6. _____ to quote exactly

**tunnel light**

B O N E S
B O N E S

JUMP

*degree*
*degree*
**degree**

W O R L D

**golf**

1. _____    the end is in sight

2. _____    a symbol for pirates and poison

3. _____    a track and field event

4. _____    questioning to get information

5. _____    extending throughout the whole world

6. _____    a small-scale game

gallon hat    gallon hat
gallon hat    gallon hat
gallon hat    gallon hat
gallon hat    gallon hat
gallon hat    gallon hat

U
P
S
I
D
E

stood

*miss*

stanyportorm

saddle

1. _____    a large cowboy hat

2. _____    inverted, wrong side up

3. _____    to get the wrong idea

4. _____    whatever refuge one can find

5. _____    a saddle designed for ladies in skirts

6. _____    in a difficult or embarrassing situation

hahandnd

angles angles angles

lives lives lives
lives lives lives
lives lives lives

HIGHWAY
HIGHWAY

jack

base        hit

base

1. _____     jointly, in union, united

2. _____     a square has four of these

3. _____     what a cat is said to have

4. _____     a road with a median

5. _____     to steal by force

6. _____     a hit that takes you to second base

**night   night**

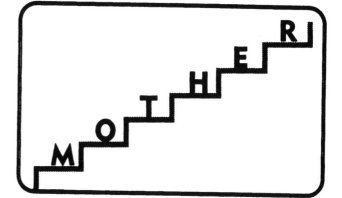

*going going going going going going going going*

**podiveol**

**FIVEQUARTER**

**working**
**time**

1. _____   the present night

2. _____   a father's second wife

3. _____   not getting anything accomplished

4. _____   one quick way to get wet

5. _____   after 5 o'clock but before 6 o'clock

6. _____   to work more than 40 hours a week

heels

empty

mermaid

water
**swimming**

eggs
eggs eggs
eggs eggs
eggs eggs eggs

good **B**
good **B** true

1. _____ a type of women's shoes

2. _____ not full and not empty

3. _____ a fairy tale

4. _____ be sure to hold your breath

5. _____ a breakfast meal

6. _____ not readily believable

earth · earth · earth · earth

WISE

talking talking talking talking talking

po **FISH** nd

your **lump** throat

**knee**
light

1. _____   far and wide
2. _____   a bold, impolite remark
3. _____   to argue without proving anything
4. _____   important among those less important
5. _____   overcome with emotion
6. _____   a non-incandescent light

Name _____

crosscaughtfire

**keep**
trying

shiningknightarmor

**cycle   cycle**

1. _____    each thing eats something below it

2. _____    to avoid answering a question

3. _____    caught between two fighting groups

4. _____    don't give up

5. _____    the hero in a fairy tale

6. _____    a vehicle with two wheels

oath
swear

gether    gether

away

white lie

M
A
E
R
T
S

**ply  ply   ply
ply  ply  ply  ply**

1. _____    promise to tell the truth

2. _____    not apart

3. _____    now

4. _____    a small untruth

5. _____    against the current

6. _____    the opposite of divide

**heavy**

C O U N T R Y S K I I N G

C O U N T R Y S K I I N G

C U P
(with T)

oneallyoureggsbasket

once

time

decker
decker

1. _____  heavier at the top than the bottom

2. _____  skiing without lifts or tows

3. _____  an alternative to coffee

4. _____  to risk everything on one venture

5. _____  a fairy tale beginning

6. _____  having two layers, decks or floors

kick

bridge

*TROUBLED WATERS*

thinvanishair

WATER

in
your head

p
o
u
r

1. _____    a soccer move

2. _____    a helpful thing during difficult times

3. _____    disappear without a trace

4. _____    a cascade of water

5. _____    unable to cope or manage

6. _____    a heavy rain

Name _____

<table>
<tr><td>field</td><td>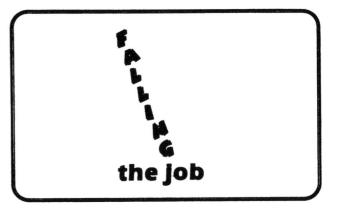</td></tr>
</table>

**field**

the job

S U N

*merry go merry go merry go merry go merry go*

*waitladying*

*CRY*
**spilled milk**

1. _____  a baseball position

2. _____  fail to do one's job adequately

3. _____  what happens every morning

4. _____  a carnival ride

5. _____  a member of the royal household

6. _____  to lament or weep uselessly

sheep'swolfclothing

K
C
E
H
C

**APPLE**

learning
**job**

TALK

*momanon*

1. _____  someone who seems good but is bad
2. _____  an examination or investigation
3. _____  New York, New York
4. _____  gaining skills while doing a job
5. _____  conversation about common things
6. _____  lunar craters

Name _____

| | |
|---|---|
| ***bopussots*** | evil **evil** |
| *whair* | arrived **TIME** |
| meal meal meal (repeated pattern) | K N O C K |

1. _____     a fairy tale feline

2. _____     the best of two difficult options

3. _____     not straight

4. _____     showed up promptly

5. _____     breakfast, lunch and dinner

6. _____     destroy or demolish

pedal

onholee

somewhere
**rainbow**

E
 X  A  I  N  E
    A  M  I
E  X        N  E
             E

priced

BE   (BE)
BE   (BE)

1. _____   to go back on or take back an opinion
2. _____   a great golf shot
3. _____   where dreams come true
4. _____   to question closely
5. _____   costly, expensive
6. _____   ". . . that is the question."

spirited

TALE

harsingmony

N
E
T
S
I
L

sun
new

BOXING
BOXING

1. _____  lively

2. _____  a story with many exaggerations

3. _____  a pleasing combination of voices

4. _____  pay attention

5. _____  everything has already been discovered

6. _____  boxing with an imaginary opponent

Name _____

| | |
|---|---|
| D<br>E<br>R<br>R<br>I<br>T<br>S |  |
| ‾‾‾‾‾‾‾ *sign* ‾‾‾‾‾‾‾ | *feet*  *feet*<br>**ground** |
| *theuonesand* | **DOX DOX** |

1. _____  agitated, aroused

2. _____  skiing on a slope; not cross-country

3. _____  what the lawyer will ask you to do

4. _____  practical, logical, sensible

5. _____  rare

6. _____  a contradiction, puzzle or mystery

Name _____

STONE

weather
*feeling*

B
R
O
K
E
N

SOAP

tuthreemenb

1. _____  a foundation stone

2. _____  sick, unwell

3. _____  not working correctly

4. _____  a platform for speaking

5. _____  a children's nursery rhyme

6. _____  something of little consequence

Name _____

| | |
|---|---|
| ___ read ___ | **S**<br>**U**<br>**N** |
| toe _____ | buckdropet |
| p i e c e s<br>p i e c e s | bit |

1. _____  to get the hidden or subtle meaning
2. _____  sunset
3. _____  to meet a standard
4. _____  an insignificant amount
5. _____  losing control, becoming flustered
6. _____  not much

Name ______________________________

haked idea

header header

n
w
o
r
g

lofallingve

behind

four
four
four
four

1. ______________________ poorly thought-out plan

2. ______________________ two games played in succession

3. ______________________ not young

4. ______________________ developing great affection

5. ______________________ forgotten, deserted

6. ______________________ a schoolyard game

e
l
k
c
u
b

BRAIN

doplayors

BEANS BEANS BEANS BEANS BEANS BEANS BEANS BEANS BEANS BEANS BEANS BEANS BEANS

jump
bandwagon

DAY yesterday

1. _____  what you do with your seat belt

2. _____  to come up with ideas or a plan

3. _____  a rainy day activity

4. _____  "Not worth a . . ."; of little value

5. _____  to take a popular position

6. _____  two days ago

thestickmud

LUNCH

Ⓛ (crossed out)

*ears*   wet

TOUCH (vertical)

SHOW

1. _____    a boring, non-adventurous person

2. _____    time to stop work and eat lunch

3. _____    a Christmas song

4. _____    inexperienced

5. _____    a football play; an airplane's landing

6. _____    not the main circus show

Name _____

| | |
|---|---|
| **beanjackstalk** | **COLLAR**<br>**HOT** |
| winks winks  winks  winks<br>winks winks  winks  winks<br>winks winks  winks  winks<br>winks winks  winks  winks<br>winks winks  winks  winks<br>winks winks  winks  winks<br>winks winks  winks  winks<br>winks winks  winks  winks<br>winks winks  winks  winks<br>winks winks  winks  winks | **calm** **storm** |
| **play   play** | *skinned* |

1. _____   a children's fairy tale
2. _____   very angry
3. _____   a nap
4. _____   unusual quiet before trouble
5. _____   two outs in baseball
6. _____   sensitive to criticism

splostace

DISE
DISE

his britches
big his britches
his britches
big his britches

c  i     i i

d
e
w
e
s

**belt**
hit

1. _____    a dreadful situation for an astronaut

2. _____    an ideal place

3. _____    arrogant, over-estimating oneself

4. _____    in total agreement

5. _____    monopolized or under total control

6. _____    to act unfairly

knock **wood**

paid
I'm
worked

teen     teen

teen     teen

teen     teen

**CAT**

i i i
i i i
i i i
i

**you
you
you
you**

fla $\begin{smallmatrix} O \\ G \end{smallmatrix}$ mes

1. _____    a superstitious act

2. _____    a common complaint of workers

3. _____    a sweet birthday

4. _____    a wealthy person

5. _____    attracted to you

6. _____    to burn up

Name _____

vicious vicious vicious vicious vicious vicious

sugar
*pretty please*

link link link link link link link
link link link             link link link
link link link link link link link

new leaf

what
*earth*

| | |
|---|---|
| one | the other |
| one | the other |
| one | the other |
| one | the other |
| one | the other |
| one | the other |

1. _____  a solution leads to another problem

2. _____  if you really want something say. . .

3. _____  a thing needed to complete the series

4. _____  make a fresh start

5. _____  a statement (or question) of disbelief

6. _____  the same one way or the other

bumming bumming bumming bumming bumming bumming

yourfeathercap

death  **life**

*mind*
**MATTER**

**better**

*burn* candle *burn*

1. _____  not doing anything in particular
2. _____  an honor or reward for something
3. _____  the hereafter
4. _____  thinking solves physical problems
5. _____  a husband or wife
6. _____  to overwork oneself

Name _____

car

ointflyment

C
A
L
M

angle  angle  angle

_____end

1. _____ a freight car on a train

2. _____ a baseball pitcher's triumph

3. _____ an obstacle

4. _____ to become quiet and tranquil

5. _____ a geometrical figure

6. _____ the finish or end of a whole process

think
your feet

glance

2 2 2 day

close
close

comfort
comfort
comfort
comfort

restdriveaurant

R
E
T
T
U
B

1. _____ to be able to think while talking
2. _____ a look toward the rear or past
3. _____ a day of the week
4. _____ a narrow escape
5. _____ a place to get food while in a car
6. _____ to flatter in order to get a favor

Name _____

<table>
<tr>
<td>

*skate*

thin ice

</td>
<td>

ward   ward

</td>
</tr>
<tr>
<td>

T
O
W
N

</td>
<td>

*round*square*peg*hole

</td>
</tr>
<tr>
<td>

in
*your head*

</td>
<td>

**line**

</td>
</tr>
</table>

1. _____   to risk danger

2. _____   in the direction of

3. _____   the central part of the city

4. _____   a misfit

5. _____   more difficulties than you can manage

6. _____   the profit or loss

**skpiey**

inside

**time**
*your hands*

e e
a a
r r
t t
h h

*fingers*
*fingers*

his **G**
**O** tory

1. _____   something unrealistic or unattainable

2. _____   reversed

3. _____   having nothing constructive to do

4. _____   practical, without pretense

5. _____   what you do when you make a wish

6. _____   to be remembered as important

**sleep**
**it**

bottom     bottom

*disblessingguise*

d
e
e
p
s

circus circus circus circus
circus circus circus circus
circus circus circus circus

stock
market

1. _____   to think about something overnight

2. _____   thorough, covering all elements

3. _____   a misfortune that turns out to be good

4. _____   to accelerate

5. _____   a circus with three acts

6. _____   when prices of stocks fall dramatically

k
n
u
c
k
l
e

o'clock
o'clock
o'clock
●

KNOT
KNOT KNOT
KNOT KNOT
KNOT

∩∩∩₀₀
COFF××

ne *friend*ed

**crawl**
**hands  knees**

1. _____  to seriously tackle business
2. _____  a precise time
3. _____  a double knot
4. _____  a pause from work to drink coffee
5. _____  a true friend
6. _____  a baby's form of movement

Name _____

piggy

zero in
it

ganightle

men | boys

s
b
m
u
h
t

keet    keet

1. _____ on the back or shoulders

2. _____ to focus directly

3. _____ a song bird

4. _____ divide the able from the less able

5. _____ a sign of approval

6. _____ a small colorful bird

# Answers

**Page 5**
1. top flight
2. once in a blue moon
3. low down
4. p's and q's
5. lunch box
6. bear in mind

**Page 6**
1. big shot
2. sewing machine
3. needle in the haystack
4. wish on a star
5. upstairs
6. ice cream

**Page 7**
1. high tail
2. 21-gun salute
3. go overboard
4. two dimensional
5. banana split
6. cross legged

**Page 8**
1. corn on the cob
2. marked down
3. you're in the doghouse
4. break under pressure
5. his eyes are bigger than his stomach
6. snow storm

**Page 9**
1. always in trouble
2. high strung
3. back to back
4. stack of pancakes
5. too cute
6. cold shoulder

**Page 10**
1. walk on eggs
2. round robin
3. saddle up
4. tricycle
5. Alice in Wonderland
6. what's on your mind

**Page 11**
1. Little Women
2. heartbreak
3. just in case
4. courage under fire
5. Big Ben
6. narrow escape

**Page 12**
1. big undertaking
2. hi ho hi ho
3. right hand
4. musical chairs
5. square dance
6. cheer up

**Page 13**
1. quarterback
2. walk around the block
3. bird in the hand
4. snow flake
5. inline skating
6. word for word

**Page 14**
1. light at the end of the tunnel
2. cross bones
3. high jump
4. third degree
5. world wide
6. miniature golf

**Page 15**
1. ten-gallon hat
2. upside down
3. misunderstood
4. any port in a storm
5. side saddle
6. backed into a corner

**Page 16**
1. hand in hand
2. right angles
3. nine lives
4. divided highway
5. hijack
6. double-base hit or two-base hit

**Page 17**
1. tonight
2. stepmother
3. going around in circles
4. dive in the pool
5. quarter after five
6. working overtime

**Page 18**
1. high heels
2. half empty
3. Little Mermaid
4. swimming under water
5. scrambled eggs
6. too good to be true

**Page 19**
1. four corners of the earth
2. wise crack
3. talking in circles
4. a big fish in a little pond
5. lump in your throat
6. neon light

**Page 20**
1. food chain
2. beating around the bush
3. caught in the crossfire
4. keep on trying
5. knight in shining armor
6. bicycle

**Page 21**
1. swear under oath
2. together
3. right away
4. little white lie
5. upstream
6. multiply

**Page 22**
1. top heavy
2. cross country skiing
3. cup of tea
4. all your eggs in one basket
5. once upon a time
6. double decker

**Page 23**
1. corner kick
2. bridge over troubled waters
3. vanish in thin air
4. water fall
5. in over your head
6. downpour

**Page 24**
1. left field
2. falling down on the job
3. sunrise
4. merry-go-round
5. lady in waiting
6. cry over spilled milk

**Page 25**
1. wolf in sheep's clothing
2. check up
3. Big Apple
4. learning on the job
5. small talk
6. man in the moon

**Page 26**
1. Puss in Boots
2. the lesser of two evils
3. curly hair
4. arrived on time
5. three square meals
6. knock down

**Page 27**
1. pedal backwards
2. a hole in one
3. somewhere over the rainbow
4. cross examine
5. high priced
6. to be or not to be

**Page 28**
1. high spirited
2. tall tale
3. sing in harmony
4. listen up
5. nothing new under the sun
6. shadow boxing

**Page 29**
1. stirred up
2. downhill skiing
3. sign on the dotted line
4. two feet on the ground
5. one in a thousand
6. paradox

**Page 30**
1. corner stone
2. feeling under the weather
3. broken down
4. soap box
5. three men in a tub
6. no big deal

**Page 31**
1. read between the lines
2. sundown
3. toe the line
4. a drop in the bucket
5. falling to pieces
6. little bit or tiny bit

**Page 32**
1. half baked idea
2. double header
3. grown up
4. falling in love
5. left behind
6. four square

**Page 33**
1. buckle up
2. brainstorm
3. play indoors
4. a hill of beans
5. jump on the bandwagon
6. day before yesterday

**Page 34**
1. stick in the mud
2. lunch break
3. noel or Noel
4. wet behind the ears
5. touchdown
6. side show

**Page 35**
1. Jack in the Beanstalk
2. hot under the collar
3. forty winks
4. calm before the storm
5. double play
6. thin skinned

**Page 36**
1. lost in space
2. paradise
3. too big for his britches
4. see eye to eye
5. sewed up
6. hit below the belt

**Page 37**
1. knock on wood
2. I'm underpaid and overworked
3. sixteen
4. fat cat
5. eyes for you
6. go up in flames

**Page 38**
1. vicious circle
2. pretty please with sugar on top
3. missing link
4. turn over a new leaf
5. what on earth
6. six of one, half a dozen of the other

**Page 39**
1. bumming around
2. feather in your cap
3. life after death
4. mind over matter
5. better half
6. burnt he candle at both ends

**Page 40**
1. box car
2. no hitter
3. fly in the ointment
4. calm down
5. triangle
6. end of the line

**Page 41**
1. think on your feet
2. backward glance
3. Tuesday
4. too close for comfort
5. drive-in restaurant
6. butter up

**Page 42**
1. skate on thin ice
2. toward
3. downtown
4. square peg in a round hole
5. in over your head
6. bottom line

**Page 43**
1. pie in the sky
2. inside out
3. time on your hands
4. down to earth
5. crossed fingers
6. go down in history

**Page 44**
1. sleep on it
2. top to bottom
3. blessing in disguise
4. speed up
5. three-ring circus
6. stock market crash

**Page 45**
1. knuckle down
2. three o'clock on the dot
3. square knot
4. coffee break
5. a friend in need
6. crawl on hands and knees

**Page 46**
1. piggy back
2. zero in on it
3. nightingale
4. separate the men from the boys
5. thumbs up
6. parakeet

## Common Core State Standards Alignment Sheet
# Word Bogglers

## All lessons in this book align to the following standards.

| Grade Level | Common Core State Standards in ELA-Literacy |
|---|---|
| Grade 4 | L.4.5 Demonstrate understanding of figurative language, word relationships, and nuances in word meanings. |
| Grade 5 | L.5.5 Demonstrate understanding of figurative language, word relationships, and nuances in word meanings. |
| Grade 6 | L.6.5 Demonstrate understanding of figurative language, word relationships, and nuances in word meanings. |